PRAISE FOR
Washing Water

Lynda V. E. Crawford's *Washing Water* is a lyrical tour-de-force. At once a postcolonial critique, an immigration narrative, a family history, and a meditation on coming of age, *Washing Water* wrestles with slavery, racism, sexual vulnerability and personal anguish. Yet in Crawford's telling, intense communal vigilance and care binds generations together in a watchful embrace: 'I tap into my mother / and she into hers / and she into hers / and on....' In the face of her newborn grandchild a woman sees 'three relatives / four ancestors... loving duppies sitting together.' Those duppies (ghosts, but more than that), haunt an old sugar plantation, a 'reminder' to its current owner of his inheritance and responsibility. Within this protective conjuration, mothers 'laugh with teeth and tongue... talk of rain while washing water' and a girl can grow up 'waiting for the sun to say, child / watch me dance in your clouds.' With this debut, Crawford establishes herself as a poet of exceptional powers.

Tom Laichas, author of *Three Hundred Streets of Venice California*

Washing Water is renewal, mystery, ritual, question: how do you wash an element that renews itself? Is it a dance, a metaphor, a passing of time? It's woman as thunder, as god, as fear and awe of her own god within–girl entering the world knowing the name she has always known. It is an offering to 'African women-ancestors across the diaspora of the Caribbean and Americas, known and unknown.' The voices renew themselves through time: 'I would sit / with my women and girls... / as they give me all / I need to know—and write.' Lynda V. E. Crawford creates documentary forms, as in, 'Drax Hall Duppies,' which hold history accountable. We receive these accounts as haunting, as record: 'This is the story my severed hand in the mill / clawed to write.' The unfolding of history also enfolds: 'see how her small arms / enfold the sky's birth water.' In receiving, we transcend.

Cynthia Alessandra Briano, Lecturer, California State University Fullerton African American Studies and Founder of Love On Demand Global

Washing Water is full-to-bursting with language that shimmies on the page while reveling in a porous world: 'it's an Earth thing', one where fore-mothers, and 'mothers who laugh with teeth and tongue', and great-grands tap into each other. This linguistically inventive debut from Lynda V. E. Crawford offers up 'such skill as you shift joy to your weak side' and the reassurance that 'Come eventide, a new nimble will settle in.' Marvel at the largesse that she brings to the lowliest: 'two raw macaroni people / with wool hair, lovingly checked / each December for weevils.' Lynda V. E. Crawford has crafted poems whose generosity of spirit are infectious, deliriously so.

Beth Ruscio, author of *Speaking Parts*, Brick Road Poetry Prize winner

Washing Water is an amazing journey to the Caribbean. Full sights and sounds of the islands—childhood adventures, practices and habits young women, mothers and grandmothers—all in the richest of language, taking us home to a place we've never been before. And, yes, when I read the collection, the voice in my head was Lynda's, in all its richness.

Karen Scott, poet

Washing Water

Washing Water

poems by

Lynda V. E. Crawford

World Stage Press
Verse from the Village

World Stage Press
Verse from the Village

Washing Water
© 2024 by Lynda V. E. Crawford
ISBN: 978-1-952952-68-5

FIRST EDITION, 2024

All rights reserved. No part of this publication may be reproduced, distributed, or transmitted in any form or by any means, including photocopying, recording, or other electronic or mechanical methods, without the prior written permission of the publisher, except in the case of brief quotations embodied in critical reviews and certain other noncommercial uses permitted by copyright law.
PRINTED IN THE UNITED STATES OF AMERICA

Cover art: *Sisters* © 2023 by Lionel M. H. Crawford
Edited by Norman Minnick
Cover Design by Mia Crow
Layout Design by Terrence Chouinard

Contact the author at lynda.crawford@gmail.com

To African women-ancestors across the diaspora of the Caribbean and Americas, known and unknown, whose hands and voices stretch through time to teach us love, and talk of rain while washing water.

To my own blood ancestors including my grandparents and parents, my sister, my brother, my sons, and my granddaughter.

To girls and women in the circle of past, present, and future.

To my forever friend Ida D. McGhee, MLS.

CONTENTS

PREFACE   XIII

I. SORREL JUICE

A Girl, Entering	3
Thunder	4
Tapping	5
I Ran in My Mother's Womb	6
Pressure	7
Climbing Trees with Boys	8
Sisters Watching Sun Clouds	9
Moratorium	10
In the Sliver	11
Chattel Houses	12
Skin-Toned: Stories I've Been Told	13
Bartered	14
Bouquet	15
Pink	16
Immigrant in Black and White	17
Afro Puffs	18
Pungent Wealth	19

II. TEETH AND TONGUE

Love in the Time of Circular Chants	23
Washing in Three Parts: 1	24
To the Girl Who Said	25
Caribbean Sea	26
Hello, Darling	27
Come, Leh We Dance	28
Ballet Is Never Enough	29
Cherries—Straight, No Allegory	30
Washing Water	31
In Conversation with Mudda Sally	32
Raindrop	33
Petrichor	34
Dada: An Incantation	35
Fire Quencher	36
Hurricane Metaphors	37
Hyacinth, in the Shower	38
Home	39

III. PEACE, SCATTERED

Mangoes	42
Hurricane Child	44
A Woman, Losing Her Lover	45
Cooling Tea	46
Scamper	47
Why didn't you tell me…	48
Washing in Three Parts: II	49
A Mourning	50
Breath	51
Keeping Quilt	52
Storage	54
Elbowing A Particular Ancestor	56
Rum and Lost Graves	58
Gently	60
Cradling the Grave	61

IV. LAUGH THE DANCE

Drax Hall Duppies	65
The Hold	67
Sweat Oil	68
Planted in Strange	69
Colonialism: An Unchecked Instinct	70
History Lesson	71
Jazz Bent the Horn	72
Dreaming A Reckoning	73
Long Enough	74
Privilege & Wealth	75
A Time Will Come	76
Shedding the Vernacular	77

V. LIFE, AWRY

About the Metaphor	81
Pelican Storm	82
The Rose	83
You Ask Me to Rewrite Rhymes and Fairy Tales	84
Yes, Great Grandfather…	85
Brine	86
Dimming the Sun	87
Ear, Distinguishing	88
Awry	89
Hatchet	90
Hinged	91
Agitation	92
Inner Eyes Closed & Opened	93

VI. WOMEN TALKING

A Granddaughter, Forming	97
Small Bites	99
A Mother's Eyes	100
Rosary	101
Avuncular (Looking for a Better Word)	102
Knowing	103
Dexterity	104
Under Skin	105
A Ring Story	106
Driving Lessons	107
Washing in Three Parts: III	108
Woman: Oysters and Dirt	109
A Woman's Body, Sometimes	110
After I Got Caught Picking Stewed Goat from My Side Teeth,	111
Women Talking, and Then She Said	112
Woman to Woman	113
What to Keep—and Let Go	114

GLOSSARY & NOTES	117
ACKNOWLEDGMENTS	121

PREFACE

I write to sneak behind eyes, blow through ears and stretch voices. I write in the belief that the love our foremothers continuously breathe into us will nourish girls and women of today and tomorrow; that any harm our ancestors caused will be washed away.

This collection is for women who've lived the fat belly of life, and understand its joys and imperfections; women who know the journey from girl into woman is one where resilience is gathered and given in laughter, dance, tears, and talk in the circle of ancestors and progeny. The poems in this collection move through this journey, with a Caribbean lilt.

Sorrel Juice

…shiver, lean far into the pull

…inhale the sorrel-juice smell of happiness

A Girl, Entering

Gurgles, babble-words
learning who we tell her she is.

She laughs as she tries to speak
that name we say she'll be called.

She pushed into earth named.
One she chose herself
or the ancestors gave her.

Suckling babe, not yet giving us
the gift of first words; unable to tell us.

She moves through her first stages
sounding us with her; we think we're guiding.

We clap and marvel:
She's starting to learn who she is!

We're without understanding.
There is a name. She has always known.

Thunder

I am thunder—in two parts.

First, rumbling, deep-voiced
to remind: I am god.

Then—I jump at the sound.

Tapping

I tap into my mother

and she into hers
and she into hers

and on

light repeated
audible blows

to

tremble, vibrate
umbilical cords

shed words

I Ran in My Mother's Womb

I.

I did not know my sister
born dead before I breathed.

When I turned eighteen
mum finally spoke her name:

Her name, my name, same name.

II.

I shiver, lean into the pull
when winds sing and rains crash

remembering I ran in my mum's womb
to escape a time-marking hurricane.

Before me, did my sister run inside mum too—
baby of the same name that I now wear?

III.

I've broken away from a tradition of cord burial
left behind in the intrusion of modern ways

I keep my sons' own—shriveled, brown, in a pouch
while mine is tucked beneath the cellar

in the island house where I was born.

IV.

I don't know much about mum's stillborn, alive
inside her so soon before me. Dear sister,

mum touched my hand and didn't say. Now I understand
my quiet; clutter my stillness to bury the thought:

I could have been my sister.

Pressure

Brass Jesus, with INRI pressed in, lived
stilled above my bedroom door six years

my mother nailed it there, to ward takers
one, a tall woman, long arms dragging — seer

in darkness, no sleep, no fear of Sundays
she came without sound; drifted through my bed

over under, exhausting in weightless flow
us, two Caribbeans — ancestry fed, bound

This visitor had pressed my sixteenth year
eager to bend my eyes toward dark light

I told my mother: *there's a darkness; please
there's a woman trying to take me*

mothers answer girls with nails, wood, brass, love

the crucifix is broken now — Jesus, dangled
on tiny brass screws, silent left palm pinned

Climbing Trees with Boys

A little girl pelts rocks, grabs gravel
snatches a boy's shoes — and she en mekking nuh sport
she adds water from the rain puddle

A little girl flicks her thumb hard
across a boy's bare head — runs down de gap in glee
flings water into a passing donkey's eyes

A teen girl plays cricket, climbs trees with boys
fun-pinches other girls' breasts and they hers
then / and only then

A mother, deep in the Lord, startles —
shakes, worries — and bends limbs
at a first daughter's need to stretch

Sisters Watching Sun Clouds

I inhale the sorrel-juice
smell of happiness

mix it with tang of cashew, fruit
yellow-fresh pulling inside my cheeks

I wrap it in the hug of raindrops
rolling off my big sister's arms

deep in my unborn power
I stretch my girlish back, buds up

waiting for the sun to say, child
watch me dance in your clouds —

big sister says: *what do you see?*
elephants rabbits tiny fish

big sister asks: *what do you hear?*
stompingtramplingboom

de devil and he wife fighting, little sis
grabble up your thunder-power

is it in the shapes of my clouds?
yes, and the crimson in your sorrow — and cloves

Moratorium

Squat and pitch
marbles.

Pinch your dress lest
the fever to scatter
an iridescent circle
of tiny glass balls,
rare to break
or chip, overrides an
inkling:

That open vaginas
can surprise semen
from virginal boy-voices
that caw each other's
names in the game ring.

Bring your own
marbles.

Clear-glass cherry seeds,
others tinged
red/blue, pink swirls;
knuckle a goochie
(a big taw). No Jacks.

Span-width the hard
mud ground to a rare
girl-win in three-holes:

before grandma drags
you in for five o'clock
tea and sweet biscuits;

before hurricane
season suspends you
under a galvanized roof;

before Nigel, losing,
skins his teeth, grins *'look…'*
and pees in the marble holes.

In the Sliver

tilt your ear
to memory
inhale the forgotten:
song of whistling frogs
tiny, on a moist leaf
blending with sound
of stars whispering
in warm night
in soft rain, after
soft rain

not the hurricane
you ran in, covered
in your mother's womb
no, not that sound

whistling frogs
open dreams at night
unlike wood doves
in morning glory
cooing love
a yearning beat

at night, little girls dream
they don't know what
don't have a name for it

it's in how grandmothers
swab sores on the legs
of dying grandfathers
how mothers
laugh, touch husbands—
such beauty in the sliver
of gold in teeth
awakening smiles

Chattel Houses

In chattel houses on
tropical islands
tiny spaces cocoon
hearty children
parents, grandparents

The legs of brothers
and sisters curl together
in a single bed
each certain the other
will send a warm flow
of pee their way

Middle girls squeeze
into parents' beds adjacent
unknowingly knowingly
parting intense hugs
unwittingly catching
lovers' dreams

Children giggle, unaware
sleeping in a room
with parents, one room
with parents, says, to some:
scarred, so poor

In chattel houses on
tropical islands
children play jacks
eat dunks, splash puddles
when rain pelts down
falls sideways
and laughter ripples up

In time, such houses
will become historic
will become others'
bought in the crush of
non-generational wealth

Skin-Toned: Stories I've Been Told

I.

A mother recalls her girl-self
denied by her pale-toned sister:
No, she's my maid

And so on   and on   and on

II.

A grandmother's clothespin pinched
small tender noses hurt red—
flat brown just won't perk pink

III.

A daughter walked miles daily
for fresh-baked loaves, sun beating darker;
now—hates bread

IV.

A mother's island face, warm eyes
soft fingers caressing cheeks, broad nose
My daughter, you were almost beautiful

V.

A light-skinned mother shuns dark newborn
I was suh sure;   no, she cahn be mine
white husband, stunned—just stares

And on   and on   and on

Bartered

When very old men with
wrinkled penises put
wide-eyed girls
on layaway;
13-year-old girls
just starting to bleed, men
wanting to be first
waiting to be first

When 40-year-old men with
agitated thoughts drive
insistent cars through
small marled gaps to
overwhelm mothers, mothers
wanting to fill holes
in their galvanized roofs
or buy their girls school books

When men with
gripping wealth take
packages of fresh fish
imported apples, cash weekly
monthly to women, women
missing their fathers
mourning their own gone men

When one man
calendars expectations while
one woman frays like
his stretched-out gray socks
& readies her only daughter

We cry for the man

Bouquet

essence of armpit
in land of upturned noses
immigrant flower

Pink

Anthurium lily tent dress
a mother's colour-hug, a perfect gift
thirty years back: puffed wide in can-can and pink joy

A flower on a twelve-year-old girl
wearing it like a cherished bucket, warm-island
watering at the standpipe; just the pink amount of swish.

From sand coral to April-coloured snow
gray highways, no flowers; but love in gabardine
topped with a kissed white hat, black velvet bow

Anthurium lily tent dress
withered rag, tucked in a land of developed noses
far from the essence of armpits flowered pink.

Immigrant in Black and White

Colour / C-O-L-O-U-R

white, chalk
across my slate, learning
fresh in the world

I chewed pieces of it
in moments of childhood urge

marking my walk, pressing
asphalt onto broken earth

I inhaled the pitch of it
in schoolgirl strolls through town

Color / C-O-L-O-R

snow, light
warm wet-fall, coaxing toes
into muddied slush

I tossed the memory of it
east coast windshield scraper in a trunk

chocolate, dark
a sea salt hint of bittering
savor in a coarse world

I parse the meaning of it
taste on my new tongue, sweetness

Afro Puffs

A Caribbean club in East Coast USA
broad stage, live band in an America where
immigrant mothers never left home without their children.

There, older men caught—and taught girls,
danced calypso like a waltz, swaying
in back-to-back hits of The Mighty Sparrow.

There, wide walls framed customs: gents in shirt-jacks,
dress pants; my mother smiling in gown-and-straight-black
Diana Ross and The Supremes wavy wig.

Me, in pant-gown, teenage palazzo puberty
swirled patterns of lilac, white, black,
1970s hair parted in, yes! afro puffs.

My 90 pounds and collar bones
perfect symmetry—deep enough to
hold a bar of soap, pull in a live drummer.

I asked my mother:
can I go for a walk with James?
She looked at us   knew   and said yes.

We strolled; I don't recall what we said
only the sweet pull of first lips;
sensed my walk back to my mother, smiling.

Pungent Wealth

I.

Salt bread and sardines
school lunch sandwich

a smell as strong as a
British teacher's accent
in a Caribbean island

as pungent as a
ruler rapping desks
when children speak Bajan

unwilling to hide
inside scabbed lunchboxes

II.

Plated silver pilchards
swirls of olive oil, fresh black

peppered elegance, curled
like hairs across napes of neck
urging us—run, cower inside

a sprinkling of Scottish clan
Isle of Skye mussels
a side of haggis, bowdlerized

away from pluck, no mashed tatties
just turnips, lamb, as art on the plate

III.

It all comes down to the letting go
to the embracing of origin oils, plaited hair

and so we laugh at ourselves—and eat
the rising cost of tiny Mediterranean fish

Teeth and Tongue

...mothers who laugh with teeth and tongue

...and talk of rain while washing water

Love in the Time of Circular Chants

Chant a psalm a day
Chant a psalm a day

An undulating Steel Pulse hosanna

That's how a Chewa man —
his ebony courting hands, soft-pressing
vinyl onto record player, evoked
a bell and bass reggae of rejoicing

A Chewa man with his budding locks
and Bantu eyes, unwitting of
church bells, Caribbean island steeples
bristle-broom sweeping the backyard
close to de donkey pen, gently
past de pigeon coop where
an old old great-woman, strong
with garlic in her bosom, stood
flinging chants of *get behind me Satan*
at bygone plantation overseers —

That's how a Chewa man
with the spin of a single record, charmed
a bursting young woman's dead grandmother
into inter-visiting, into whispering into her ear:

Marry him, I want to be his in-law.

Washing in Three Parts: I

I was a washing machine
little girl squishing boadicea blue
school uniform in juking board and tub

before my wrists were strong
before I learned to suck in
I stood in that tub, belly free

grandma pouring fresh water
over my head, rain-falling my back
rinsing me after a good scrub

To the Girl Who Said

drink a beer—with this ice cube numbing,
you won't feel a thing…

I felt a thing:
felt the ice seize & burn

as we laughed; she couldn't grasp
how I reached twenty-one;

didn't have my ears pierced.
she pushed needle-threaded

white cotton through one ear, another
I sipped more beer—told her:

make more holes; help me twine the
gold of my grandfather's teeth

garlic of my grandmother's bosom
girl in my mother's smile, elbow-tall gloves

glint of my father's firefighting badge
all the way through my new woman.

when she was done, I was ready
to purchase spirit, shift

from girl songs in my ears
to nostril breaths centering me.

I cupped my own sharp-tip rose gold
self-piercing circle ring

shaped to accent curved corners & pressed
a smile into my ancestral nose.

Caribbean Sea

Odd, that I once thought
making love in the sea
would ebb and flow like
warm waves with a hint of
Georgette Heyer gentility
buoying us...

Even our ancestors *know* better —
know clenching in Caribbean seas
soothes sweat, washes come into waves
gushing and lilting with laughter
that crosses the ocean, past Cape Verde
towards a hint of Africa, undulating
stronger than any Victorian novel...

We're back in ourselves
un-alone on our pink-sanded beach
watching gleamed-skin boys sneak
high-up coconut trees to remind us:

We have to pull out of this sweet salt wet
drench our sand-matted hair
quench our mouths' thirst
smile at seawater everywhere...

Hello, Darling

earthy funk, mushroom
musk of underarm

a nose curls into
a lover's pit

legs curve across
a rested phallus

both loves soothed
into silence, babies forming

in such moments
sleep soon comes

Come, Leh We Dance

calypso, kaiso, ringbang, soca

merge horns into morning cock crows
tingle pan, pound bass

wuk up our waistlines
in a giggle first, then

a sweaty laugh

Ballet Is Never Enough

For Caribbean girls who want to point toes
tighten, lessen their backsides into the unnatural
stretch to strings of violins—having lost the kora

For Caribbean girls who strain to keep arms above heads
pirouetting away from ancestral earth skin

Be wise

Listen to your mothers who laugh with teeth and tongue
watch them grabble flared poplin dresses
above their knees; gyrate hips into a curved spoon-bowl
a cycle of earth life, circle of star life

Be carefree

Follow *Mudda Sally,* caress fertility ripples blue/green
clear from across the ocean
of your future, your past, your present musk life
look askance at small-bone-breaking dances
that bend and bleed phalanges

Be swift

Push past advents: Spain, Portugal, England, France
push past interims: kompa, kalenda, bele, kaiso
wuk down into deep dance—a dingolay
on a sea path to reclaim your original wombs

Cherries—Straight, No Allegory

Unlike his office mate—
fresh mix of American brash & ebony silken hair
who, with unaided dexterity, could tongue-tie
the stems of cherries into precise forbidden knots—

his at-home wife
of untampered peppercorn curls, pink-brown lips
& short lingual frenulum at birth, couldn't untie her tongue
to wipe warm sweat from the tip of her nose.

But, she could fuck in horizontal gyrations—
a rhythmic ringbang dancing clench.

So, he kept his tongue-tied wuk up wife
& together they threw away the rest of the cherries.

Washing Water

I would sit
with my women and girls

I would flow
through generations

to listen while they
stir cou cou as women do.

I would sit
with them on mats of straw

as they give me all
I need to know—and write:

how to scrub away old bubbled-out suds
how to rinse in play-tossed pampalam

and talk of rain   and laugh
while washing water

In Conversation with Mudda Sally

Let me charm you with my backside
gorgeous rise of stretch marks, formed

as I rushed into puberty and beyond

See how my pink coral shells couple
with cowrie, curving in to cup me

watch them jiggle with my smile

Notice my belly, smooth. Twice
cocooned babies in pure cocoa butter

full of child and no darkened prize lines

Don't hold that against me. Front stria
the proud-new-mole-on-her-right-cheek

beauty mark. That's not for me

my splendour lives where I sway
Mudda-curved to guide   or mamaguy

Raindrop

I stepped inside a raindrop today
took time to find its perfect wet

shed days, rain jacket, gray hood

I moistened the curved width of my nose
caressed its warmth and beaded scent

tasted time, ancient thoughts, brownish pink

it was easy to sway out of myself
touch where I made the rain drop

Petrichor

dark rare street-wet
hoodies move in fitful pace

four floors up soft plop on sill
I can't see the raindrops

I grasp the smell of rain
in a child's laughter

drift to earthy musk
stomped mud puddles

steel pan slant on tin roof
the ping of muted mallet

mizzle lands on moist slugs
sits a moment on a girl's lash

see how her small arms
enfold the sky's birth water

how grown-ups hunch
shoulders deep in memory

Dada: An Incantation

if mama in the grave
one fore day morning

digs far past her rock stones
pries your tomb's shiny metal

to tap your stiff left shoulder
she's trying to tell you:

I need seven-guidance &
unbroken wrapped arms

soothe me in seawater
tell me of those amniotic days

when I curled stilly in her womb
teach me to swim in power outside

Fire Quencher

blending wind & road, sirens whining
past cars asleep in the streets
blaring by tents of unhoused men & women

so many cocoons: some neon new, most faded
homes of choice, not of choice, of last choice
fire engines & ambulances, coming & going

screaming awake the night, jarring the dawn
some days I mute them into distant horns
at the intersection of my ear & childhood

where saviours of bodies & houses move
in communion with water, island hoses, pick axe
firefighters weighted by pounds of lifesaving

my father sliding the pole
in an urgency found only in
insistent gods

Hurricane Metaphors

Pelt
when an island grandma
pelts bible words over de paling
a neighbour is hit with a storm

Slice
galvanize torn
roof song after island storm
childhood memory-rain

Wound
a named hurricane
pushes rain sideways
disturbs a pregnant womb

Release
intensity of hurricane winds
a whorl of indiscretions
lovers beg forgiveness

Hyacinth, in the Shower

She tosses her short afro as if a long-tressed ancestor moves
unburied, inside her. Her name is:
Hyacinth-of-a-Vincentian-Mother-and-Scottish-Father.

At 13, she longed for GoGo boots—useless on a hot island,
her mother said—a mother whose mother and her mother curved,
swayed to bale notes of sugarcane.

Remembering at 17 the want of an electric toothbrush,
Hyacinth imagined the zing of it, how she tried to smoke a cigar—
stuffed it in the larder to keep her youth pristine.

She inherited her father's father's nana's wool-loving eyes, strolls in
island heat naked, her desire to orange-yellow the brightest white linen
shirt-dresses buried; her swirl dreams of bronze/blue, pastel pinks for sale

in a discreet shop left dimmed with her regret—she should have braved
water, learned to surf when her dad bought the board.

At 25, Hyacinth loves to bend with her girlfriends' ways—posh Vincy
bohemian brash by day—then settles her breath nightly, catching
her new husband's groans, his highland-croft moans of tricked,

enslaved ancestors; never mind her own, yoked. He's a civil servant—
his rhythm timed to reach Scotland, find the family his forefathers lost.

In the shower, she still holds her breath, frightened of drowning when
water hits her face. Her name is:
Hyacinth-the-Essence-of-Vincentian-Spice-and-Scottish-Lace.

Home

Home heat-wraps
its two arms around me from the front:
murmurs giddily
girl, gimme a good belly wine.

I sweat gyrations:
Faluma, Pump Me Up
Peter Ram's *Good Morning.*

Home coaxes
moistened accents into the curves of my lips:
massages my earthy thoughts
and whispers to remind me _____

I inhale notes:
Nuestro Tema, Red Curbs Loop
Carrington: Outside Looking In.

Home tremolos
in entwined tender tones, guttural sounds:
plaits Yoruba, Akan, Taino
and Carib into my island tongue.

I breathe timbre:
of mothers, brown-skin uncles
ebony great grandmothers.

Home washes me
in sounds heard and hummed
before my birth:
the call of whistling frogs
my wood dove's faraway coo.

I enfold
night rains and
soothing glory this page cannot contain.

Home makes me wonder why
all of Earth   cannot be…   like this.

Peace, Scattered

...winds pushed and dragged rain sideways

...our sense of peace, for a time, scattered

Mangoes

Mangoes drop down
from trees, the weight of

their ripeness too much
to stop the motion, too

heavy to shun the lane
where a baby sleeps

in a pram, waiting.

Hurricane Child

Born frightened, always ill & rubbed in camphor,
I saw my mother's hand sew a white infant burial dress.

As winds pushed & dragged rain sideways,
I sent my sister before me; saw her hum the patter too soon,

disturb the womb & our mother's hitched breath;
stop the family dinner song.

I replaced her — the one who, curious at the storm, startled
& stilled, never to see our mother's life & death, nor cocoon

in the stir of cou cou & underskirts of our family's circle dress.
I lived — thrived on stories shared of hurricanes & names.

Long past mama's death, I remember a wooden cradle
darkened by unpainted years.

A Woman, Losing Her Lover

grandfather dying
and grandma pulling she hair
it real short and gray

and she crying bad bad
and sitting and vomiting
and clutching up she guts

hollering 'Oh God'
'cause grandfather dying

I seeing everything
but I so young, I so scared
I can't figure out why she doing all that

is only grandfather
grandfather riding he donkey
grandfather baking bread
grandfather giving me a penny...

grandma scaring me
I wonder how come she crying so hard
she must know something I don't know

Cooling Tea

The distance flows tall
as a grandmother's right hand
moves up in a tight bond
with her cup. Enamel,
slightly chipped.

A down flow of milk tea
descends to a partner cup
bringing soothing air
to cool the heat,
save tongue from burns,
leave room for sweetness.

A child's eyes look up
at the tea fall's soft guttural hum,
grandmother's gnarled fingers
strong as the habit of a juniper tree,
a pencil cedar, gone and unforgotten.

How many times
have strong brown wrinkles
of left hand echoed right,
left cup rise, with a child
counting each pour aloud?

Hands know when it's time.
They've since passed, yet
memories still pour.

I stand in my grown-up kitchen
hear the suctioned release of fridge door
opening to take in a single hot cup, to cool.

I keep still. Wait.
Watch a thudding close,
remember a tall distance
when a grandmother's hands flowed up.

This tea, cooled by electricity
appliance, gasket, a closed door
fails to soothe my longing throat.

Scamper

Were you running to freedom
when you dashed through the door

a tiny black body nursed
from birth—not by your mother
soft white teeth falling out as
I pushed a bottle of cow's milk in?

You must have needed one scamper
into space unstressed
from the weight of curried oxtails
chopped onions, browning

un-trapped by walls that separate
living from sleeping, cooking from eating.

I cried for you, my bleeding pup
in my clutch, shitting unknowing
across my gut, your back crushed.

In the moments before brakes crunched
we were both happiest.

Why didn't you tell me...

before you walked down the aisle in your wedding gown, face pinched
before I blurted out *he's a narcissistic creep*
before you smacked him in the head for neglecting the kids
before you scissor chopped your hair after you touched your breast
before I laughed, chided *girl stop,* thinking you were joking
before I had to ask your doctor what palliative care means
before you swallowed the drug that took you away
before I jumped into your grave and hollered, stalling the final hymn

Washing in Three Parts: II

The laundry room is there
washing machines are there
well, one. The other, perpetually broken
notice stuck to its top—warning
of leaks and failure to drain.
The other works; isn't left wondering
how children will be fed
what to do when the Tap Card expires
or when a distanced friend gleans clothes
piled in the back seat
are not donations waiting to join Goodwill.

A Mourning

Thunder rents the sky / tears a hole
destroys our sense of peace

winds and rain drive us, frenzied
into hurricane whiplash

our deep wet will come / tears will spill
enough to pour through our devastation

our sense of peace — for a time — scatters

Breath

I'm taking back my inhale pattern
given during vows.

I can sleep, almost soundly —
turn sideways at the foot of our bed

point my toes, push my chest up, outward
breathe in out in out — breathe.

I can sleep like that
or roll to the innermost cup of the mattress's dent

where years of sweat, breast milk, sweet semen
collected; formed the tightest bond.

He's dead — years of my breath taken
to his village in a steel box, blue on wheels

to people who wail strongest, bring rain clouds
down to soak thirty years of unnatural breathing

I'm taking back my exhale pattern
paused during vows.

Put him in the ground now —
let his ancestors breathe in, out in unison.

Keeping Quilt

What have I to do with quilts?

My American friend—the one who
picked up my school books when
I dropped them at my locker, frightened
at the rush of feet; the chatter, so far from
island secondary school where children sit
orderly in classrooms, chatting quietly
mostly readying for new knowledge
while teachers walk to them
upright-bosom-strong, firmly, from
class to class, around square corners
no rushing into small hallways—
my American friend who always loved
a crochet needle, or making squares for quilts
like her mother and so many ancestors
before her—she would understand the gift of a quilt.

But I am perplexed.

This stitching together of
memories, events, patchings of flowers;
what does it mean? What does it beget?
When my African husband was dying of cancer,
my next-door neighbor, having given up
on urging me to church, walked over one evening
with a square-shaped cloth—padded offering
of black squares, tan squares, darker tan squares.
such quietly-toned beauty, suited to the soft pale
of our den's furniture; not the carnival red core
of my soca-arcing waist; not the kwasa kwasa
librating through my hips—and my once ebullient husband's.

I unfold the quilt.

Soothe my finger along the stitching
on the back, I read: 'Blessed Pray Quilters.
Each knot represents a prayer said especially for you.'
There's a tiny box shape with the number 1213 inside.
Hand-marked? Stenciled? A pattern indicator perhaps?
And a heart shape surrounded by a gift-of-love date:
August '08. It too seems hand-marked.

But what do I know of quilts?

And about the date; no — that's not it
my husband died in June of '09.
This is the only quilt I have.
I won't donate it with my long-worn blankets,
my dead husband's many suits, shoes.
And I won't quilt. I wouldn't dream of
stepping into the patience it requires.

Storage

*No one noticed
she didn't leave each night
didn't leave that night*

Moonlight registered
her ritual visits, knew
she no longer locked
and looked back, knew
she had downsized

Five by ten, down from
suburbia's ten by fifteen
a unit that had already sighed
parted with four-inch heels
VHS tapes, suits with piping
no longer worn

A unit that forgot
there once was more:
a yard embracing
a three-car tract home
that bragged loud

Faux Victorian pale-blue
couch graced with baby's pee
ink, milk-spit

Panels of books rich, obscure:
The Adventures of Joseph Andrews
The Cow Tail Switch
a heavily pencil-marked
History Will Absolve Me

New coffee maker
in a stained box
giver unknown, unremembered

Children's grades
gap-toothed photos
memories ruckled
in a jumbled pile, hugging
each night as she hugged back

Ornaments, in peculiarities of two
two sons; similar, not matched

Two raw macaroni people
with wool hair, lovingly checked
each December, for weevils

She wore a mask
life-hardened to her face
from years of use
went where she went
hiding in front of estranged
family, friends

She died in her bin
one moonlit night
curled adjacent to her pots
storage money still owed

Elbowing A Particular Ancestor

I.

Sending a deliverer of cuts
by false knife... I mean to say
sending mama those divorce papers isn't
      I'm coming right back

II.

My father, your eyes cried silently watching
my eyes, I heard you say I'll come,
the curve of your mouth hugged me a 'don't cry,
      I'll come right back'

III.

You hope to rest undisturbed, my ancestor
your own mother in her step-up
veranda'd island house, scoffing 'he behind he nose'
when mama calls to ask. Rest is not to be.
      You didn't come right back

IV.

We trembled with you — children, shocked
into America's April-gray cold confusion
at our mother's enterprising; pulled from moist
breeze and Sunday lunch.

V.

You brought us to her. Were you reluctant?
Emigration, a step-down from lieutenant fireman?
To what, you wondered.
You could not stay... and a teenage girl waited
      You didn't come right back

VI.

But a father/daughter love is un-breaking
Oh! Susanna Oh don't you cry for me
who taught me that song
helped me learn to read?

VII.

Who wooden-ruler'd my hand
when my brain didn't subtract? Who sat me
on his lap as I loved the Lakeland
water color set. I idolized you, dada

VIII.

See us. Sit up in your death.
See your grown children striding
in matching black to cry at your burial
my love is un-breaking

IX.

The Twelfth of Never...
that song you mellowed in
You ask how long I'll love you
a song to push my heart to the wall
near your coffin; fractured eye water

X.

*Until the twelfth of never
I'll still be loving you.* When you died we
caught the last plane in a blizzard, landed into worse
Death delivered you into deep cold—in April.
It's the cruelest month someone once said.
Ancestors pulled you under.

XI.

I'm ready to chat. Stop liming—let's talk.
No under-graveyard fires to quench? Too many?
I'm nudging you. But not to pay my school fees—Ah!
I see, you thought I forgot. And I've made you smile.
I'm smiling too, although…
        You didn't come right back

Rum and Lost Graves

Dear father, I have sinned.
I have not stretched my ears

in days; have not called the voice
of my uncle from his grave—

that boisterous gusto
of our mother-mirror,

the uncle I tried to match in
grog-for-grog dark haze.

Linnie come fire one with me
he always charmed his niece.

Uncle, you are your favorite sister.
We bury her tomorrow.

Dear earthly father of ours, I have sinned.
I should have visited you more.

You don't know your first wife's dirge
on such a burst of dwarf poinciana day.

I mean our mother, father dear.
Twined gold. Bright blues.

Hand-painted dresses all around.
And uncle in despair:

Can't find the grave his mother/father share.
We should have let you dip, uncle who could not find

your sobered grief; a grief defined through centuries
where plantation great relatives cant.

Dear father, I have sinned.
This struggle to write each day. I tried

to write of dark rum and loss;
snot yellowed from the lineal nose

of a little one who sucked her fingers swibbly,
left the earth too soon.

There's more, my uncle: Stop shouting to
our grandparents as they doze;

the ones whose grave you always found
with drink and sober heart, unerring gait.

They're busy chatting with your sister.

Gently

he hummed gently—rubbed the song
into the curve of her neck
kept bile from giving birth in her throat

Cradling the Grave

but as I was saying...

some of us heard her laugh
others imagined that mischievous smile
we were doing the same, in a pause from sighing
between hymns we haven't sung since we left
some not sung since island primary, secondary

ancestor amongst pink satin, rosary in hand
we placed it there when we opened the casket
saw her hands had risen, waiting
long-rubbed crystals with silver cross
we had gently twined it between her fingers

but as I was saying...

some of us ourselves laughed
others mirrored her mischievous smile
in a pause from funeral—a dirge
wanting to squirt blood from heart
in a pause from frangipani tears, eyes rubbed raw

which spirit will plant enough ginger lilies, hyacinth
create a hug in the opened space between her children

but as I was saying...

in a pause we heard her giggle
cuh dear at our cousin's first song—a sound scraping ears
and the second, serrated; cousin, don't make us belly-laugh
not in this cemetery where we bend to cradle the grave
don't disturb the rest of the mischievous

Laugh the Dance

...an ancestor was packed tight, salty in sweat oil

...until I laugh the dance, the story has not been told

Drax Hall Duppies

*A reminder to Richard Grosvenor Plunkett-Ernle-Erle-Drax,
British MP owner of Drax Hall Plantation, Barbados*

I.

erasure was complete—or so we thought
individuals, names drowned along with tribes
suffocated in stench of slavery; mutilated
in the grind of sugar cane

Royal-owned enslaving ships, coining and abusing;
self-named aristocrats preening in plantation
scarring and burning alive; ash-ing our lineage

II.

erasure was complete—or so they thought
we didn't know of Caribs, Arawaks, Taino
severed from Fulani, Hausa, Dogon, the Igbo
medu netjer—hieroglyphs far across the sea

we were generations-of-no-eyes, silently booed
those who started to see: like George Lamming
he spoke the word *African*—claimed continent as kin

III.

erasure was complete—or so we were taught
we feared twentieth-century speech
at our national stadium during a day of CARIFESTA
us, Little England, raised high on false buoys of Britain's

ancestors—those who tacked, jibed, laughed at the sound
of our folly; mumbled *fools* under breath as we preened
in falsehoods, ignorance, molasses, and grog bliss

IV.

erasure wasn't complete—and our ancestors don't forget
we may have stiff-upper-lipped the whole: dark plantations, weighted
heavy with power: breaking bone, drawing blood, burying blood...

not anymore; we honouring forebears in public spaces
names known: Bussa, Clement Payne; some lost...
our duppies are churning under sugar cane; hundreds—roaming de place

V.

they holdin' history, wuking obeah, markin' dah trail
from parliament tuh plantation—and back.
wuh is dah yuh say? 'It has nothing to do with me'. All dah family history?

Your James Drax, Prince of Barbados; 600 acres, 300 Africans first time out?
hear wuh ah say Lord Richard: we comin' fuh yuh
remembuh: you cahn rub we out.   Erasure   dun....

Drax Hall Plantation, St. George, Barbados where the first sugar cane was cultivated in 1642

duppies: ghosts, spirits, ancestors

Richard Grosvenor Plunkett-Ernle-Erle-Drax inherited Drax Hall in 2017.

George Lamming (1927-2022) Barbadian novelist, poet, academician

CARIFESTA (Caribbean Festival of Arts)

Bussa's rebellion (14-16 April 1816) largest slave revolt in Barbadian history. African-born enslaved man named Bussa

Clement Osbourne Payne (1904-1941), trade unionist; led rebellion against the planter class

The Hold

My husband snores loudly, sometimes
rumbling into me as earth's upheaved crust

I pinch his nose, hold holes together
stopping the sound before it rolls into a sea-crash

holding   holding   holding
in blissful silence, still not sleeping

I don't know how many of our ancestors
pinched their own, slipped overboard, determined to return

I count how long it will take him to sputter
take me to stop my own deprivation—and sleep

Sweat Oil

canned sardines
in olive oil
having emptied the fish
poured liquid
oiled satisfaction
into my throat

it kicks in

not in my hippocampus, a place
we're taught holds memory

not in my temporal lobe
processing, encoding

it kicks in

controls where I live
and sweat
my heart rate
blood pressure
breathing
swallowing

it kicks in

an ancestor of mine
was packed tight
salty in sweat oil
and for a moment
could not breathe

Planted in Strange

This is the story I will tell you.
Come back tomorrow and I will tell it again.

In the time   before now
we pleaded to the oceans:

Gnash your wave throats
against our salty calves

where we stand planted in strange.
We can't hear you, my ancestors

your drums muffled in seawater.
We dreamed, captured you in oil drums

muted the steel of our pan to soothe
our children into lullaby   hold their breaths.

This is the story I should tell you:

We were human, once. Ancestral names
known. Fused with land and life.

Then, we were money.
Currency traded for long guns.

Chattel. Beam of Real Estate. Asset-in-new-lands.
Insurance to keep the cotton, clothing.

Collateral to kings. Sugar's birth mother.
This is the story my severed hand in the mill

clawed to write, curled to hug the Voodoo
inside the Obeah inside the Orisha inside me.

Until I laugh the dance, the story has not been told.
Come back tomorrow and I will tell you.

Colonialism: An Unchecked Instinct

The speed of my hand
as it picked a nearby
holy card, swiftly
smashed it down
on the head of a fly

I am stunned by the still
the silver sheen near its eyes
the black of skin

I register the saved savor
still-warm sweet tea
touched by the white
from an unknown cow

History Lesson

It's in how she exhaled
and in so doing, pushed
evil through her pale teat
suckling her fair-eyed babe
her own uterus tightening, careless of
a nearby collectable postcard,
a lynching caught
in her fleeting glance
a glance that would seep, feeding
generations to come.

Jazz Bent the Horn

like Harriet charmed the moon
to sleep at her will; make a way
when the eyes of her people called.

I imagine her chant—her demand
un-breaking, marking a circle of ancestors
across centuries before and centuries after.

There was a time before we were offered
dragged; before we landed afar, anew
& couldn't always run.

Is that keening a familial call
from across the seawater; a message
bending sound with us?

We need to open our ancient eyes
& chant-awake the hundred billion
nerves that make us human; hear our

ancestral navel strings—once buried deep
rise & sing, eager for our return. Let them conjure
with us—forge a new jazz to deliver us from this.

Dreaming A Reckoning

That ugly thought—

    / we are a caste perpetual, beneath their feet /

could have been vomited
into your ear my love—or

tamped into our family circle-stress
deep enough to coalesce inside us.

Instead, we rejected inculcation
propelled truths into the air, crowded

with thousands marching, pressed up to polymer
power of the state, helmets—firm in our persistence

to cast out systems that keep us in self-doubt
& rob & rob & keep on robbing us of ourselves.

We've stopped fearing government guns
& covered noses unwilling to inhale our prescient smells

but destined.

Long Enough

I heard a leader say
we can wait—
long enough for you to die
and for your children to forget

I heard a different echo
we will wait—
long enough for you to die
and for your children to forget

I heard the children's children singing
a reckoning song
long past the jumble of history
and memory's attempt to recast

Privilege & Wealth

Slavery bought it.
Law maintained it.

Children of chattel built it.
Children of owners inherited it.

Houses were acquired using it.
Universities gained, claiming it.

Presidents ascended power hiding it.
Valiant deaths through generations, challenged it.

Centuries of tipped & bloodied weighing-scales
buried deep in a nation's cursed DNA — cement it.

Millennials benefit while not understanding it.
Black men are imprisoned, locked from it.

Imbalance thrives in its descent — & dissent.
Poverty & desperation are crushed under it.

Slavery brought it.
Laws maintain it.

Few believe
reparations will resolve it.

A Time Will Come

First   the scoffing
while African-descended ones purge
protest, pick at inner pain.

Then   the eating of piles of fear
excreted from a lifetime of swallowing
slithering, sliding away.

Next   the shooting & lynching
enslaving & clutching of pearls,
even faux, will restart.

Finally, if gods care, we will murmur
together, find the lost sounds buried
deep in our shared oceans.

Shedding the Vernacular

neck shackles   and whips

that's why *Umbundu* dimmed crossing the seas
why *you is wunna*

how *Twi* hid in Caribbean cane fields
then crossed to birth *Geechee* amongst blows of cotton fields

how *gwine* and *gine* and *gurl guh long*
sashayed into *wid cho bad self*

how we jived back across the ocean to
hold hands with *Amandla! Awethu!*

spirits unbowed   shedding the vernacular

Life, Awry

...I cannot swim a fairy tale

...what is lost in ocean brine will never feed new flies

About the Metaphor

This is not it, me
upside down, behind my nose

mouth whipping black-inked strokes
pen-eyes dripping

Pelican Storm

Storm in the Mountains pulls me.
A tree? A pelican
once strong and bright,
brown, with toes and beak in sand
and trident blues all around.

An island home of its own
now gone. I stare, cast
my eyes down, following my buried bill.
A Pelican Island merged. A national bird.
And pelicans mostly gone.
A tree, lightning-split. Dead.

This mountain is not an island.
A tree is not a pelican.
Barbados is not Connecticut.
How did I get here? Tossed.
My vibrance paled to amber?

The thrashing of water foam
against the out juts. Where is the sand?
Lightning, dancing with hurricanes
(or mountain storms), can bend a pelican's back.
Or crack the verve of my oak. It's the same pull.

The Rose

nothing smells
like America
sweat purged
dream-concept limp
her national rose
struggling
to breathe deep
inside the power
of countless
cherished scents

You Ask Me to Rewrite Rhymes and Fairy Tales

To such, I can't devote my cherished twinkling time
tomorrow you will want a gibberish of rhymes

and next you'll vex me with your glee, ask me
to re-imagine an undefeated dumpty humpty. I say Shoo fly

don't bother me...I'm in glow of my new cataract surgery
my right eye in love and awe of how I now see.

*How now brown cow...oh no siree, don't distract me
don't turn my head upsided down wid a cup a dah cocoa tea.*

Follow my hand as I stretch it lightly up into the blue.
Float after my fingers tingling in softened cumulus dance.

A beckoning—let half of me run-twirl and spin
and spin and curl inside the sky as never danced before.

See bright dimensions unimagined—the other half of me
in idle rest, flat upon the beach in grins, squish of toes in sand.

*If all the seas were one sea, what a great big sea that would be!
So many cockles and tiny shells for Sally to sell by the shore.*

Is that a hint of orange glow, a sway of eyes enframed?
A peek of dancing red in blue of flame as I direct my aim

ignite a pot of gas-boiled wet? A steeped chrysanthemum, tea
more crimson than a song of ocean waves forever crashing?

I cannot swim a fairy tale: island girls back then not taught to swim
nor boys jumped into the sea and moved like fish and never drowned.

*Adolphus   Adolphus   gimme piece
I guh tell yuh wuh happen—pappy kill 'em, pappy kill 'em.*

I will tell it all in time; time in tea and deeper newer eyes.
For now, don't speak to me of reinventing nursery rhymes.

Yes, Great Grandfather...

I've turned Emily over; crept inside her.

It is her fault I hear the flies buzz, smell one crawl
along my bony toe — suck my left armpit of enemy
lymphatic nodes. I see its cousin flit along my shoulder blade,
futile, in search of dead & drained old blood. The first fly says —

bend your elbow farther back — dare to scratch
that embedded itching sound. My arm contorts & I dream
of nails & boarded louvres; of schools where children hide
from historic island wind & storms that split our memory-time

Then — I remember. I am not dead.

I am the girl who watched in black & white, saw Tarzan swing
dear Jane. I pleased my mother with my words of want: I want
to be the native ones whose firm dark feet rub Mother Earth.
I want my hair to be — as short & tight as seed-peppered black.

I'm ready to slash Jane & her man. They are in my way. I hear
the other fly belch — the one still fat with blood of the small boy
who died of leukemia in my tropical island home. I ask that fly:
Why can I see this boy's face & no longer know his name?

It does not have an answer.

I turn on my side & seek my grandfather's father whose face
I cannot see. Great grandfather says: What is lost in ocean brine
will never feed new flies. Find the flies your forefathers ate.

Brine

A small sea
keeps me cocooned
slightly salted
forgives me
for unlearning

Dimming the Sun

Four point six billion years old.
I have yet to absorb this number. And, it will change.

I have yet to fully know the nature of ancient rays,
how I revolve around their heat and shine;

Why I'm here. Why my home is here.
How many are we now — eight billion? How that will change.

Are we as knowing now as those who bled our bodies?
Leeches in the fullness of healing — until, with wisdom, we stopped?

Or just as knowing as those still frozen in cryogenic thoughts
who hope to live again? To eat and sing with those yet to be born?

Are we as knowing as those who kindly drain our blood — cleanse
and cycle it in quick time through our diabetic bodies?

Replace our dying hearts with those of pigs, still beating. And what?
Transplant our eyes with others' corneas to make us clearly see.

Each practitioner always right until we, and they, are wrong — or right.

Keep seeking wings to fly — not melted wax and feathers gone from Icarus
who died in want to touch our ever-brilliant sun.

We've made the ripstop nylon strong; felt the promise of freedom's wind.
Yet, so far, we have not come so far.

I saw a headline: *Dimming the Sun to Cool the Planet…*
and so, I write today what, tomorrow, will surely be wrong:

> eight billion screams
> and millennia from now
> our dust and starry eyes
> will squint at our bright sun
> reflect the ever-urge to dim
> and laugh at our fated folly

Ear, Distinguishing

the sounds of water

heaven's amnion rain, coats the earth
—the skies clear

city hoses splay last night's detritus
—the sidewalk clears

an ear

once cocked to sing with faraway stars
lies with its body against pitted concrete

distinguishing the difference in

the sound of water

Awry

Michael inhaled,
archangel, ragged
still bleeding tears
for the pet dog
strangled.

He exhaled
a soft hum,
remembered
a soothing day
when he sat on a
bench, alone
in his favorite
museum.

On that day
thoughts of white puffs
cumulus against blue
pulled him in

On that day
he stared
into the bright red clutch
poppies, brilliant
oil on canvas
a painter he never knew

He remembered the gurgle
could almost smell the red

Hatchet

I miss-see the point
certain oil strokes
dreams leaking from tendrils
fingers that spill onto wood—or
that wide daub on canvas

I miss-read the goal
of an unseen sliced ear
drop of soothing pearl
roughened death mask
carved to spirit my praise

Even Marshall's
Portrait of Nat Turner
with the Head of his Master
fails to keep me focused
mindful of ekphrastic

I ease into graphite
smooth-trip into poem
chasing an altered form
as stark images pose near
not shaping my words, yet

I hear them bleed
sliced, through my fingers
my hand no longer a rose-paled tip
no, not that. Now, I am the hatchet

Hinged

Dried, wood without moist
yesterday we were the barn

in want of snowmelt to wet
our seams / just a little

no mold no slow dripping mess

a river, barely, had flowed
in our hearts all day, unknowing

of mounds, nearby snow
caressed grass not yet gone

not fully in its winterness.

I was ignorant of your wanting
you, unquenched hard in rebirth, fire

of your mother's thighs; a river
confined, its path not meant for me.

You could have been a tree, majestic.

I should have been your fir, prolific
formed of a thousand seeds, breathing

life into our barn's hinged door.

Agitation

When his car went in de gully
the car she sacrificed food tuh buy
he remembered she had foretold it

tried to tell he doan drive that night
mind you—not so as to keep his sperm
tuck up inside he tuh save it fuh she...

No, she warned him, to slow him down
cause him to live—not die in de dark-night
maybe   brek up he car, not he body & soul

alert to his spirit guide inside her, a spirit
insisting she guard him with words
she had opened her eye and forewarned him

now, he blaming she fuh hexing
fuh wuking obeah tuh mek de motorcar
guh down de gully hole—fuh purpose.

Inner Eyes Closed & Opened

once, when I was dead
I breathed deeply, free
now I am above ground

I can't walk long through ancient graveyards / the ones in Caribbean slow winds & sunshine / without hearing "yes girl chile, we listenin" I start talking / answering / sweeping away dust / whisper to the coral and limestone / I'm uncertain how the cradling will end.

I don't walk slow through pristine cemeteries / at least not more than once no one whispers to me there / no friendly voices of mothers, grandmothers great grandfathers & their sisters / cemeteries with taller-than-six-foot headstones mark cold climes / Europe / interims pushing upwards for permanence.

I won't walk deep through crypts / above grounds / under grounds / I slip fast away from cold moist dank / catacombs that claw to return me to a dark place where I once died / that is not for me / what dragged my ancestors' ancestors & their ancestors' ancestors deep / must not once more pull me.

I will walk strong through pyramids / Mer of limestone, granite that insists I descend / press fear down / I haven't yet learnt to breathe in narrow tunnels / long passages / longer memories / in the name of opening my inner eyes to kingdoms and foregone grace.

Women, Talking

...a mother's eyes, when opened in the back of her head

...just enough vernix on skin to glory in play and sound

A Granddaughter, Forming

did you ever
inhale
look
into the eyes
of your grandchild
still becoming
see three relatives
four ancestors
lola nanay
flicker by
in out
hear them
murmur
& wonder
are they
contemplating
debating
agreeing
which one of us
will settle in
for a moment
for a while
which one will
sort out her walk
how her elbow
will akimbo
whose tint of voice
will enter
stay
deepen
when her bambo's
birthmark
that strawberry blush-rise
on her belly
will fade
into her great granny's
departed
timbre of voice
& spirit

how her
not-yet-known
mga apo
will sing
how her agogo
now cradling her
& so many
loving duppies
sitting together
legs outstretched
on mat of straw
will shape her
keep her safe
did you ever
look
wonderstruck
in recognition
in that instant
see into her universe
say darling
your smile
for a moment
I saw your grand aunt
your lola tiyahin

Small Bites

My mother's smile seeped, most often
through her slanted brown eyes

into the space in the middle of my head,
under the bones in the middle of my chest
in between my toes — and caressed me.

On rare days, she had two boiled eggs:
one for my father, the other she moved
from mouth to mouth to mouth

of her three small children,
nudged each one of us to   *bite*
something she could do with hens' eggs

never pigeons'. I didn't know to ask then:
mama what will you eat

A Mother's Eyes

A mother's eyes
when not in the back of her head

when not catching you at this or that

can see under your armpits
smell the sweat of your woman burgeoning

& slant into a smile; say *I remember too*

A mother's eyes
when not in the back of her head

when giving life lessons about this or that

can wink at your waistline, teach you
how to clutch up your dress in a circle beat

& dance-call your great great gods into kaiso

A mother's eyes
when opened wide in the back of her head

when protecting you from this or that

can blind an inclined man preying your way
pierce him with a *not my girl chile, you too old fuh she*

& wrap you in her hug-tight bond; say *I remember too*

Rosary

I keep a rosary
in a cup holder in my car.

When I'm in trouble, worried
for my sons, the world

I rub it if I'm near,
think of it if I'm far, compel it

to bring answers
that I can make work for me, for them.

Its Jesus and Mary carry
no meaning to me, yet

these beads have the power
to help me know which right is right.

It is my mother's.   left.
I pray to her.

Avuncular (Looking for a Better Word)

I tap an email on my mobile phone,
incoming from Word Genius, Word of the Day.

Said loudly, its second syllable expands my chest. Avuncular.

I strain to remember the meaning
before looking. I always do.
Rotund, jolly, effusive perhaps.

I'm wrong: *Affection and kindness from an uncle.*

I have many uncles
all dead on my mother's side
some on my father's, alive.

I don't spend time with them.
When I was a child they hinted strongly
of higher status than my mother.

My favorite uncle, Eddie
was gorgeously thin, brown-skinned
strong-voiced; always laughed
with a hint of a scratch
sounded like his sister, my mother.

My favorite aunt, Golda sat
on the sand at the beach—
or was it in the yard near our pigeon coop
was there a pigeon coop—
to sing songs, tingle our young ears
with tales of dinner dolphins caught in fishermen's nets.

When her baby son died, of pneumonia
before a year, before my awe
at tiny human bodies faded,
her long tears flooded her shirt; stained into me.

I want a word for her.
What is kindness and affection from an aunt?
Materteral is not what I expect.
I'm looking for a better word.

Knowing

She turns off location
services on her iPhone,
grabs a just-sautéed plate ...
of chicken feet
left over from dim sum
with year-round friends;
settles to
Adventures of Sherlock Holmes
an old British series running on someone's
YouTube channel

Friends know
the gal who slurps oysters
with champagne,
the studied senior who
glides through museums,
certain to wear the whitest
shirt, flared sleeves; the
tattered jeans, years-faded

She knows
sucking soy sauce-tinged gristle
from such tiny feet is as tasty
as feasting on the archaic
word that pushed last week's
poem to perfection; knows
the pleasure of teeth removing
every bit of seasoned flesh
leaving so many tiny bones, bared

Dexterity

A scraping of knuckles as your hand grabs

a catch of metal spikes, edges rounded to shield.
Sixsies and Sevensies. Can you feel your swiftness?

The sweep and swoosh to take in all life has to give
before your tiny bouncing ball drops?

Such skill as you shift joy to your weak side
free your public palm, grab a descending star

in a moment of risk. Can you catch that falling sun?
Sixes and Sevens? See how you buy dexterity

with less-tried aims. Your imbalance of grip
dust covering your fingers, knees scrunched, toes bent.

Just enough vernix on skin to glory in play and sound.

You were yearning for the new world's promise:

no more heavy water pails at the standpipe
pad on head, stiff spine, limber neck

no miles to walk for loaves of bread
only your breath, fresh in power, luck in fist.

Did you know a day was entering: drawstring-in-bag-and-plastic
your jacks game tamed, frisk gone, your joy snatched?

Old jacks in tin cans capture breadfruit and fish cakes, fat pork
and period blood of puberty swooping in laughter, reveling

in rub of prize against palm. Youth gripped in glee.
Come eventide, a new nimble will settle in — find you scraping

always abrading; woman, cutting, contriving, surviving.

Under Skin

through eyes rinsed fresh by tears

a peculiarity will slow-slide, squeezed
from yellow drips of ripe mango

rushed from memories of who you sweated
against a coconut tree; rough-husked & hefted.

when your eyes check for stars

a pull of words will scrape through your teeth, tart
from tug-pick seeds of golden apples

glide smooth from what you once hid under skin:
old worries oiled down in lessons learned.

A Ring Story

Never let your mother tell you who to marry,
my mother said. I imagine her devilish laughter:
Should she wring my father's neck,
search the small marled gaps
to fight a brood of squawkers lined up to peck?

(No, don't blame the women, mother said.)

I forgot to ask you, mama:
what happened to your ring? Was it lost
in the throes of headless flight—
divorce the same as a plucking of feathers,
hands in hot water, a still-warm body?

(Yes, and I don't blame myself, mother said.)

In my own youth, my fingers slipped, unsteady
as I tried to slit a neck for supper.
Something went wrong. I still dream of the fowl cock—
his body running headless. Grandma caught him.
Made curry chicken.

(Yes, I remember, that was a good supper, mother said.)

Driving Lessons

The lieutenant fireman sighed.
His young, short-haired wife begged.
They had started marriage with kids
like so many couple's pegs.

He was raised to think entitled,
she came swaddled in temerity.
Her pinafore framed struggle,
his knit shirt a posh family.

She tried for status by adjacency,
steadfastly cut and contrived;
bought the box-shaped navy car
to bolster his public pride.

Mother, wife, she dreamt
of sunny family excursions
while he gave lifts, ice cream sprees
to afternoon diversions.

His pledge of driving lessons left her fed up,
mocked her redundant pleas.
He always forgot, she always remembered
every blasted word, by degrees.

Through louvre windows on afternoons
her small children watched, waited.
She considered their lesson,
restarted plans she had once vacated.

She moved her children to America,
soon taught herself how to drive
left foot always on the brake,
measured self-power derived.

Washing in Three Parts: III

Who is to sort bag, basket
arrange colors, materials—light, heavy
open a lid, drop in detergent, choose cycle
cull hard-to-find quarters that banks once alerted
we're running low on coins

The machine keeps time—agitates
absorbs piles of sweat from shed skin
hair, hints of truffle oil
wayward scales of a striped bass, stuck
to sweaters mingling with summer tees
in the odd season of pandemic

Woman: Oysters and Dirt

like perpetual grinding of sand into pearls
somewhere there's a next, a woman kindest

One sleeps at night
on angel-decked pillows
in a downtown loft. Smiles
most often while slurping oysters
from their ocean shells.
A glass of fine wine, sometimes.

The other sleeps night or day
on concrete gray
in a coat the color of muted dirt
on rotation: sleep, stroll, ask
disappear to return—to press once more
onto the hard horizontal.

One gives inadvertent twenties
tens with hesitation; fives most often
wrapped in small talk, risking
the day they each might speak names.

The other gives deliberate hours
to waving, following, then...discerning:
one dollar bills speak loudest
pushing her to less tried blocks.

A Woman's Body, Sometimes

sweat-moistened suction
pulling in laughter

home to long pubic hairs, curled
in familiarity between fingers

a woman's body, sometimes:

site of a fowl-sized fibroid
dropping clots in unexpected places

plea for return of underarm fuzz
after purged lymph nodes ...

a woman's body, sometimes:

strolling, un-cupped from wires
uneven right breast singing

a woman's body, sometimes:

lyrical resting place
happiest sprawled

After I Got Caught Picking Stewed Goat from My Side Teeth,

having said I ate steamed bok choi, fresh fish
with white onions and garlic, and told you

there's nothing wrong though
one breast was sucking in chemo to kill cancer,

I'm not sure what type of lies I tell.
I used to say I only tell big lies. You know.

The kind big enough to protect you — and family. But.
Sometimes I tell little lies. The ones to ease our paths.

To let me slip by unnoticed. Those to pause your tears.
Make your day set and rise. Ones we'll both forget.

That I'll forget — and get caught in.
Actually, I don't remember which types of lie I tell.

Women Talking, and Then She Said

I walk like a girl

I walk worried
about the group of men sauntering towards me

I walk like I'm in love
laughing with the eyes who watch me, urge me on—and wish

I walk wistful
yearning to get back to a planet the Dogon *just know* we came from

I walk in the rain
trying to lick drizzles from my lips, taste wildness in me

I walk sleeping
seeking to make sense of thinking, to make sense of making

I walk dancing
swaying my arms and botsy like a twirl of clouds wrapped in reggae

I walk slowed
at the thud of earth hard on the box, denting to shield grace from theft

I walk relieved   I walk running   big woman striding

I walk   like I'm in charge

Woman to Woman

When two women who know
who *see*—who *are* each other

two women who know
& understand the fat belly of life

two women who breathe in & cherish
how their mothers'   mothers'   mothers…

When dem two women hear balangalangalanga
gut power of that age-old brake drum call

that circular tire iron beacon sounding
on de main road & start tuh wine up pun each other

botsy to botsy   planet   tuh planet
sweet pan rotating in de universe

When two women who know, get up
& start an unforgotten chant—it's an Earth thing

a 'we-navel-string-bury-right-hey' ancestral ting
& if yuh doan understand wuh we saying

    get out we way.

What to Keep—and Let Go

At 5 years I heard a wood dove sing and grandma translate—
ooh ooh   ooh   ooh   ooh   Moses speaks   God's   word

I soaked up the haunt of her Redifusion, wired relay
Herbert W. Armstrong's radio show The World Tomorrow.

At 16, on a bus ride home from school
steeple bells rang, tolled my grandma's voice near

reminding of her '69 trust pressed strongly onto my youth:
No man can go to God's moon, they've gone to Israel's Mount Zion.

Did she smile when my ears released her clang-song of bells
or sigh in peace to hear my lips lilt toward our shared bird song?

At 30, I kissed such sounds into the moyo of my husband. Abambo
did you hear her guiding life into her children—into us and our sons?

In my 40s and 50s I dreamed—stayed her clothespinned hand
remembered how it clasped forced tradition, pinched my broadened nose.

I long ago chose what to keep—and let go
how to overcome tainted false history and the Cross.

At 65 I joined old and young in a cheer of Perseverance
marking the span of immigrant curtilage from shed roof to Mars.

I've discarded grandma's translations, wrong words
keep her coo—and the wood dove's soft yearn-song.

GLOSSARY & NOTES

ABAMBO: *Chichewa* — a respectful form of father

AGOGO: *Chichewa* — grandmother

AMANDLA! AWETHU! *Xhosa (South Africa)* — power is ours / power to the people

BAJAN: language of Barbados (mixture of primarily British English and West African languages)

BALANGALANGALANGA: sounds of triangle instruments when repeated by people during Carnival

BAMBO: *Chichewa* — father

BELLY WINE: *Bajan* — to dance

BOTSY: *Bajan* — derriere / bottom

BREK UP: *Bajan* — to break something

CAHN: *Bajan* — can't

CARRINGTON: *Outside Looking In: Composition* by Michael Nyman from the movie *Carrington, Outside Looking In*

CHANT A PSALM A DAY: the song *Chant a Psalm* by Steel Pulse

CHEWA: short for Chichewa (one of the many languages of Malawi)

COU COU: Barbados' national dish (yellow corn meal with okra)

CUH DEAR: *Bajan* — commiserate sympathetically

DIMMING THE SUN TO COOL THE PLANET... partial headline of story that ran in *The New Yorker,* November 2, 2022

DINGOLAY: Caribbean term for dance

DOAN: *Bajan* — don't

DUN: *Bajan* — done

DUPPIES: *Caribbean* — ghosts, spirits

EN MEKKING NUH SPORT: *Bajan* — serious, not joking around

FALUMA: the song *Faluma Ding Ding Ding* by Alison Hinds

FUH: *Bajan*—for

FUH PURPOSE: *Bajan*—intentionally / on purpose

GOOD MORNING: the song *Good Morning* by Peter Ram Wiggins

GINE: *Bajan*—going

GWINE: Jamaican—going

GUH: *Bajan*—go

GURL: *Caribbean English*—girl

JUKING BOARD: *Bajan*—old-time ridged wooden board used to wash clothes by hand

KAISO: modern form of Calypso

LIMING: *Bajan*—gather together to socialize or have a party

LOLA NANAY: *Tagalog/Filipino*—grandmother on the mother's side

LOLA TIYAHIN: *Tagalog/Filipino*—grand aunt

MAMAGUY: *Caribbean*—to deceive or tease, either in jest or by deceitful flattery

MARSHALL: American artist Kerry James Marshall

MGA APO: *Tagalog/Filipino*—grandchildren

MUDDA SALLY: a Barbadian fertility character traditionally performed by a male in a mask but today is performed by unmasked women with stuffed sacks to exaggerate bosoms and bottoms

NAVEL-STRING: *Bajan*—umbilical cord

NUESTRO TEMA: the song *Nuestro Tema* by Silvio Rodríguez

PAMPALAM: *Caribbean English*—delight at another's plight (can be playful)

PELICAN ISLAND: a former tiny island off the west coast of Barbados where brown pelicans nested. It was merged into the mainland in the mid-1950s during construction of the Bridgetown Port. The brown pelican is the national bird of Barbados.

PUMP ME UP: the song *Pump Me Up* by Krosfyah

RED CURBS LOOP: the track *Red Curbs Loop (Stuff I Dream About)* by Teebs

REDIFFUSION: wired relay radio. Barbados was the first British colony to have the service in 1934.

REMEMBUH: *Caribbean English* — remember

RINGBANG: a Caribbean musical fusion form credited to musician and producer Eddy Grant

SOCA: one of the modern forms of Calypso

STORM IN THE MOUNTAINS: 1847 oil painting by Frederic Edwin Church

SUH: *Bajan* — so

SWIBBLY: *Bajan* — severely wrinkled, grayed fingers (typically caused by excessive sucking)

TING: *Bajan* — thing

UMBUNDU: a Bantu language

VINCY: casual reference to a citizen of St. Vincent and the Grenadines

WID CHO BAD SELF: *African-American* — with your hip, wonderful, all-powerful self

WOOD DOVE: *Barbados* — a bird similar to the mourning dove; makes the same cooing sound

WUH: *Bajan* — what

WUK UP: *Bajan* — to dance (involves gyration of the hips)

WUNNA: *Bajan* — you plural

YUH: *Bajan* — you

ACKNOWLEDGMENTS

With gratitude to the following literary journals where my poems (or versions) first appeared:

ArtsEtc Barbados: "Love In The Time of Circular Chants", "In Conversation With Mudda Sally", "Shedding the Vernacular"

California Quarterly: "Cradling the Grave"

Crosswinds Poetry Journal: "Breath"

Exposition Review: "Ballet Is Never Enough"

Haikuniverse: "Bouquet"

Inlandia's These Black Bodies: a chorus of Black Voices Anthology: "Dreaming A Reckoning"

Mayari Literature: "Dimming the Sun"

Moonstone Arts Center (various anthologies): "Long Enough", "Driving Lessons", "Women Talking, and Then She Said"

Prairie Schooner: "In the Sliver" reproduced from Prairie Schooner Volume 97, Number 1 (Spring 2023) by permission of the University of Nebraska Press. Copyright 2023 by the University of Nebraska Press.

Quantum Entanglement: "Storage", "Rosary"

Rue Scribe: "Mangoes", "Come, Leh We Dance"

Spectrum Publishing: "Caribbean Sea", "Hello, Darling"

The Caribbean Writer: "Pressure", "Chattel Houses", "Bartered"

The Dead Pets Poetry Anthology: "Scamper"

The Galway Review: "Drax Hall Duppies", "Cooling Tea", "Avuncular (Looking for A Better Word)", "Why Didn"t You Tell Me…", "Tapping"

The Halcyone Literary Journal: "Knowing", "Avuncular (Looking for A Better Word)", "Cooling Tea"

Special thanks to Beyond Baroque Literary Arts Center's Wednesday Night Poetry Workshop, Community Literature Initiative (Sims Library of Poetry), Eastern Shore Writers Association (ESWA), Viva Poets, Los Angeles Writers Group, poet James Evert Jones, Merano Writers, Poetry Apocalypse, and all of my colleagues in poetry.

Lynda V. E. Crawford was born and raised in Barbados and lives in the United States. Both homes sway and punctuate her writing. Crawford writes to sneak behind eyes, blow through ears, and stretch voices. She's been a journalist, copywriter, website manager, and email marketer. Poetry won't let go. Her work has appeared in national and international print and online journals and anthologies including *Prairie Schooner, ArtsEtc Barbados, The Caribbean Writer, The Galway Review, The Bookends Review, California Quarterly, Exposition Review, Spectrum Publishing, Moonstone Arts Center* (anthologies various), *Crosswinds Poetry Journal, Los Angeles Poets Society Los Angeles Poets for Justice: A Document for the People Anthology* in honor of George Floyd, and *Haikuniverse.* Her poem 'Ballet Is Never Enough' was nominated for the Pushcart Prize and the Nina Riggs Poetry Award. Crawford is a graduate of The University of Connecticut (Bachelors) and Long Island University (United Nations Graduate Certificate) (Masters).

www.ingramcontent.com/pod-product-compliance
Lightning Source LLC
Chambersburg PA
CBHW060530080526
44586CB00012B/688